NEW VANGUARD 337

TANKS IN THE GULF WAR 1991

STEVEN J. ZALOGA ILLUSTRATED BY FELIPE RODRÍGUEZ

OSPREY PUBLISHING

Bloomsbury Publishing Plc

Kemp House, Chawley Park, Cumnor Hill, Oxford OX2 9PH, UK

29 Earlsfort Terrace, Dublin 2, Ireland

1385 Broadway, 5th Floor, New York, NY 10018, USA

E-mail: info@ospreypublishing.com

www.ospreypublishing.com

OSPREY is a trademark of Osprey Publishing Ltd

First published in Great Britain in 2025

A catalog record for this book is available from the British Library.

ISBN: PB 9781472864758; eBook 9781472864741;
ePDF 9781472864734; XML: 9781472864765

25 26 27 28 29 10 9 8 7 6 5 4 3 2 1

Index by Alan Rutter
Typeset by PDQ Digital Media Solutions, Bungay, UK
Printed and bound in India by Repro India Limited.

Osprey Publishing supports the Woodland Trust, the UK's leading woodland
conservation charity.

To find out more about our authors and books visit
www.ospreypublishing.com. Here you will find extracts, author
interviews, details of forthcoming events, and the option to sign up for
our newsletter.

Title page image: see p. 6

Key

(-) indicates a battalion etc. which was understrength

Author's Note

The author would like to thank Stephen "Cookie" Sewell for his help with
Iraqi tank markings and Christopher Foss for supplying several photos for
this book. Unless otherwise noted, all photos in this book are from the US
Department of Defense and its organizations.

CONTENTS

TANKS IN THE GULF WAR, 1991

INTRODUCTION

In August 1990, Iraq invaded Kuwait in a lightning attack spearheaded by tanks. The Kuwait invasion threatened neighboring Saudi Arabia. The United States, Britain, and France joined Saudi Arabia to create a coalition to oust Iraq from Kuwait. Saudi Arabia pressured a number of Muslim countries to join, and eventually, more than 30 nations took part.

Saddam Hussein could not have chosen a less favorable moment to foment war in the Gulf region. With the end of the Cold War in Europe, the NATO nations had a substantial force that could be mobilized and transported to the Gulf, based around the US Army's Third Army in Germany. The 1991 Gulf War saw the greatest tank battles since World War II. Both sides possessed more than 5,000 tanks each.

DOCTRINE AND ORGANIZATION

The Iraqi Army

Iraqi Army organization and doctrine was strongly influenced by their long contact with the British military before and after World War II. Their initial organization was patterned on the British General Staff model, but gradually diverged in the 1980s due to their experiences in the Iran–Iraq War as well as growing Soviet and Warsaw Pact influence. A distinct variation from the British pattern was the establishment of a Republican Guard Force Command (RGFC). Although this initially began as a small force to protect the Ba'ath Party dictatorship, it eventually evolved into an elite combat formation.

Tactical initiative in Iraqi Army operations was handicapped by the centralized control of Saddam Hussein's crypto-fascist Ba'athist regime. Decision-making was heavily centralized in Baghdad, and the paranoia instilled by the regime encouraged tactical commanders to strictly follow orders and avoid personal initiative or flexibility. The

A Polish-manufactured T-55 of the Iraqi 16th Armored Brigade, 6th Armored Division, knocked out in its revetment during fighting with the British 1st Armoured Division. The eerie dark sky was the result of oil fires deliberately started by Iraqi forces as a means of concealment from Coalition air observation.

Iraqi Army, as in most developing nations, lacked an experienced and trusted NCO cadre that has always been the backbone of any technical combat arm such as armored forces. While this type of authoritarian command-and-control tradition proved adequate against the slow-moving and equally inept Iranian Army in the 1980s conflict, such rigidity was poorly suited to a fast-moving war of maneuver of the type that the Iraqi Army confronted in 1991.

A typical example of the consequences of Saddam Hussein's centralized control occurred in December 1990, when Lt Gen Al-Nu'ami, an experienced commander of the Iran–Iraq War, was sent to review the Iraqi deployments in Kuwait. He reported to Baghdad that the divisional commanders had a poor appreciation of their assignment, troop morale was poor, and desertions were high. He concluded that the forces in Kuwait could not withstand a Coalition attack for more than a few days. Infuriated by this honest but grim assessment, Saddam sent a civilian deputy, Izzat Ibrahim, to review the troops. Needless to say, he reported back that the Iraqi troops were in fine fighting spirit. The Iraqi defenses in Kuwait were based on such delusions.

In the 1950s, the Iraqi Army was equipped mainly with British Churchill and Centurion tanks. This Churchill Mk VII on parade in May 1957 was named after Saif al-Dawla, the most prominent member of the Hamdanid dynasty and the founder of the Emirate of Aleppo in the 10th century.

There were three standard Iraqi Army divisions: armored, mechanized, and infantry. Nominally, an armored division was based on two armored brigades and a mechanized brigade, while a mechanized division had two mechanized brigades and an armored brigade. Infantry divisions were generally based on three infantry brigades and usually included a tank regiment for support. Armored brigades generally consisted of three armored regiments and a mechanized regiment.

The Republican Guard Force Command (RGFC) was a praetorian guard for the protection of Saddam Hussein and the Ba'ath Party. Its military element originally consisted of six independent brigades. In contrast to the regular army, the Republican Guard were volunteers and were recruited based on loyalty to the regime. In the early phases of the Iran-Iraq war, the RGFC served as an operational counter-attack force and was used to crush Iranian offensives. The superior combat performance of the RGFC convinced Baghdad to greatly expand the RGFC so that by the spring of 1988, it formed its own corps with several divisions. By August 1990 at the time of the invasion of Kuwait, the RGFC included eight divisions and about 32 brigades. The RGFC traditionally received the best equipment and had priority for supplies. For example, a regular Iraqi tank unit would have T-55, T-62, or Type 69-II tanks while a comparable RGFC unit often would have T-72 tanks.

A formation of T-62 Model 1972 tanks of the Iraqi IV Corps in the Basra area during the opening phases of the Iran–Iraq War in the early 1980s.

A large number of new M1A1 tanks were shipped to the Kuwaiti Theater of Operations in the fall and winter of 1990 to replace older M60A3 and M1 tanks that had previously been deployed there with their units from Germany. This Abrams is testing its smoke-generation system, with a growing white smoke cloud behind.

In a defensive engagement, Iraqi tank units preferred to fight enemy tank units from static positions due to the limitations of their crew training. When the terrain permitted, Iraqi doctrine favored reverse-slope defense, with the unit positioned down the opposite side of a ridge or hill. The aim of this tactic was to ambush an enemy tank formation as it crested the hill or ridge, at which point the lead enemy tanks could be picked off by the stationary Iraqi tanks positioned below. At the same time, following waves of enemy tanks would have no ability to locate and identify the Iraqi tanks until after they had crested the hill, at which point they would still be vulnerable to Iraqi fire. This tactic minimized the tactical shortcomings of the Iraqi tankers, such as poor gunnery training, and placed minimal demands on the crew. The gunner would be instructed in advance of the range to the target, so the gun could be battle-sighted to engage at a predetermined range without the need for range input data which would slow a poorly trained crew. To improve their survivability, Iraqi tanks were often deployed in shallow revetments constructed by combat engineer units, which reduced the vulnerability of the tank hull to enemy fire and minimized the target presented to enemy gunners. The use of prepared defensive positions was especially common in the regular army divisions along the Kuwaiti border. In general, the regular Iraqi Army was more comfortable in a defensive posture.

A significant shortcoming in Iraqi Army organization was its inadequate and outdated air defense network. The Iraqi Army did not fully appreciate this issue prior to the 1991 campaign, since the Iranian Air Force had posed such a limited threat in the Iran–Iraq War.

Some Iraqi tanks, including this Type 69-II, were fitted with a set of pipes leading from the left-side exhaust port to the front of the vehicle to enable the tanks to create smokescreens while in revetments.

The Iraqi predilection for a defensive operational approach was very evident in the 1991 Gulf War following the short-lived Khafji raid. The Iraqi Army deployed in a succession of defensive positions along the Kuwaiti frontier. The initial layer of the defense was a linear formation of infantry divisions along Kuwait's southern frontier. These were backed by a layer of armored and mechanized divisions. Although Iraqi doctrine indicated that the role of armored and mechanized divisions was to conduct counterattacks, the actual posture was much more static than the doctrine proposed. The third and final layer was the operational reserve of the RGFC divisions, which were intended to conduct mobile counterattacks against any breakthroughs of the previous lines of defense. Baghdad had greater faith in the ability of the RGFC to conduct maneuver tactics than the inadequately trained and weakly motivated conscript troops of the regular army divisions.

Coalition forces: US tank units

The United States CENTCOM (Central Command) provided more than half of the overall Coalition tank strength. The US Army deployed 29 tank battalions and six armored cavalry squadrons, while the US Marine Corps provided five tank battalions. There was also a large tank reserve afloat in the Gulf under the US Navy.

The US forces were distributed in three principal commands. To the far west was the XVIII Airborne Corps, which included the 24th Infantry Division (Mech) as well as two airborne divisions and other units. The heaviest concentration of US tanks was with the US VII Corps, located immediately west of Kuwait's southern border. This contained the 1st and 3rd Armored Divisions, 1st Infantry Division (Mech), 1st Cavalry Division, 2nd Armored Cavalry Regiment, and other units. The third US formation was the I Marine Expeditionary Force (I MEF), which contained the 1st and 2nd Marine Divisions as well as the Army's Tiger Brigade (1st Brigade, 2nd Armored Division).

The US Army maneuver divisions were generally organized into two or three brigades. The armored divisions' brigades typically included three to four battalion-sized task forces (TF). These were usually combined-arms formations including tank companies, mechanized infantry companies, or cavalry squadrons. For example, TF 1-35 Armor of the 2nd "Iron Brigade," 1st Armored Division, consisted of three tank companies from 1-35 Armor as well as a company of the 4-7 Infantry (Mech). The mechanized infantry divisions had a similar organization, though the ratio of Abrams tank battalions and Bradley mechanized infantry battalions was different, with only four tank battalions in the infantry divisions versus six in the armored divisions, but correspondingly more Bradley battalions. The two armored cavalry regiments each had three armored cavalry squadrons, mixed formations of Abrams tanks and M3 Bradley

When 4-64 Armor, 24th Infantry Division (Mech), first arrived in Saudi Arabia in 1990, it was still equipped with the M1 Abrams tank with the baseline 105mm gun. It converted to the M1A1 Abrams prior to the start of the ground campaign.

A Marine tank crew have set their cots alongside their M60A1 RISE (Passive Applique Armor) named "Lefty." While one crew member takes a nap, the rest are behind the tank doing maintenance on its AVDS-1790 diesel engine prior to the start of the ground campaign.

Cavalry Fighting Vehicles. The 82nd Airborne Division had the 3-73 Armor attached, equipped with the M551A1(TTS).

The two Marine divisions in the I MEF were reinforced and were generally organized into multiple combined-arms task forces. Their tank battalions were generally dispersed within the task forces in company-sized elements. For example, TF Papa Bear of the 1st Marine Division had three battalion-sized elements consisting of the 1/1 Marines, 3/9 Marines, and 1st Tank Battalion (-). The 1/1 and 3/9 Marines included a company of AAV-7 amtracs (amphibious tracked vehicles) and a tank company from the 1st Tank Battalion.

Coalition forces: UK tank units

The principal tank element of the British forces during Operation *Granby* was the 1st Armoured Division, which served in VII Corps. This included the 4th and 7th Armoured Brigades. These were combined-arms formations consisting of armored and mechanized infantry units. Generally, an armored regiment battle group would have an attached mechanized infantry company with Warrior IFVs, while the mechanized infantry battalion battle group had an attached tank squadron with Challenger tanks. For example, in the 4th Armoured Brigade, the 14/20 King's Hussars (-) had a company of the Grenadier Guards, while the Royal Scots had an attached tank squadron from The Life Guards. There were three armored regiments in the division, either on the Type 43 or Type 58 pattern. The number referred to the quantity of tanks in the regiment; the Queen's Royal Irish Hussars and The Royal Scots Dragoon Guards were the Type 58

A Challenger I Mk 3 tank of the Troop Leader, 4th Troop, A Squadron, Royal Scots Dragoon Guards, 7th Armoured Brigade, advances in Kuwait on February 28, 1991. The diamond-shaped device on a pole at the rear of the turret is a TOGS (Thermal Observation Gunnery Sight) indicator for A Squadron to permit neighboring tanks to identify its troops at night.

configuration, including a Challenger tank in the headquarters squadron, four saber squadrons with 14 Challenger tanks each, plus a reconnaissance troop with eight Scorpions.

Coalition forces: French tank units

The principal tank element of Operation *Daguet* was the 6e Division Légère Blindée (6 DLB, 6th Light Armored Division) that served in the XVIII Airborne Corps. It included a single tank regiment, the 4e Régiment de Dragons (4th Dragoon Regiment), with 44 AMX30B2 tanks. The remainder of the division included a mixture of mechanized infantry and cavalry formations.

Coalition forces: Saudi–Arab coalition tank units

The Saudi military included armored units from the Saudi Arabian National Guard (SANG) and the regular army under the Ministry of Defense and Aviation (MODA). The SANG was the praetorian guard of the Saudi royal family. Saudi Arabia led a wide variety of units, mainly from neighboring Arab countries, but also including other forces such as those from Pakistan. Many of these forces were small, symbolic deployments. Some of these national units saw little if any combat action.

The Saudi-led Joint Forces (JF) were positioned along Kuwait's southern border and consisted of two commands: Joint Forces Command-North to the west and Joint Force Command-East along the Gulf coast. These two forces were divided by the US I MEF in the center.

JFC-North consisted of three main elements, including the Saudi–Kuwaiti Task Force Khalid, the Egyptian II Corps, and the Syrian 9th Armored Division. This command had the largest contingent of Arab tank units. TF Khalid contained Force Muthannah, with the Royal Saudi Land Forces' (RSLF) 20th Mechanized Brigade plus the Kuwaiti 35th Mechanized Brigade, and Force Saad contained the RSLF 4th Armored Brigade and Kuwaiti 15th Infantry Brigade. The Egyptian II Corps included the 4th Armored Division and 3rd Mechanized Infantry Division. The Egyptians fielded 531 tanks in nine battalions. The Syrian 9th Army Division was the principal reserve

An Egyptian M60A3 (Passive) of the 3rd Armored Brigade, 4th Armored Division, in Saudi Arabia in December 1990 prior to the start of the ground campaign. It carries the division's lion insignia on the turret side.

of JFC-North but saw little or no combat action in the ensuing campaign. Pakistan provided a number of units under Forward Forces Command Ar'ar, including the 7th Armored Brigade. This force was deployed to the far west of the Coalition forces beyond Rafah and does not appear to have taken any role in the fighting.

JFC-East was a mixed Saudi–Arab force, including units from the UAE, Kuwait, Oman, Bahrain, Qatar, and Morocco. There was a screening force along the border from the Saudi National Guard. There were four Task Forces – Omar, Othman, Abu Bakr, and Takir – each consisting of an RSLF mechanized infantry brigade with other mechanized infantry and infantry elements from the coalition. This force had substantially fewer tanks than JFC-North.

In total, the Saudi-led forces deployed about 27 tank battalions, including 9 Egyptian, 6 Saudi, 7 Syrian, 2 Kuwaiti, 2 Pakistani, and 1 Qatari. As mentioned previously, neither the Syrian nor Pakistani units appear to have been significantly involved in ground combat, and so are not covered in any detail here.

 M60 TANKS OF THE JOINT FORCES

1. M60A3 (Passive), 8th Ministry of Defense and Aviation (MODA) Brigade, Royal Saudi Land Forces. Saudi tanks were usually very plainly marked, with few if any distinguishing insignia. They were painted in overall FS 30372 Sand or the similar CARC 686 Tan according to US sources. The usual Coalition "^" marking can be seen on the turret side. This insignia was adopted after the Khafji fighting to reduce the problem of fratricide and was supposed to be carried on all Coalition vehicles. Saudi vehicles usually carried the Saudi flag on one of the radio aerials. Another result of the Khafji fighting was the decision to use orange air recognition flags on the top of tank turrets as a means of air identification, a practice that had been used by the US Army since World War II.

2. M60A3 (Passive), 3rd Armored Brigade, Egyptian 4th Armored Division. This shows an M60A3 in typical Egyptian camouflage consisting of a base sand color with sprayed bands of olive drab and earth brown. The tank carries the lion's head insignia of the 4th Armored Division, with the red/green circle indicating the 3rd Armored Brigade. The vehicle number "134" is carried in Arabic numerals on the upper turret side. This tank lacks the usual Coalition "^" insignia, which wasn't applied until after the Khafji battle.

1

2

TECHNICAL FACTORS

Iraqi tanks

The Iraqi Army had been equipped with British and American tanks until the July 1958 military coup that overthrew the Hashemite monarchy. In 1959, the new Iraqi military dictatorship signed an arms agreement with Moscow, initiating three decades of Soviet arms sales. The first deliveries began in 1959, and by 1961 totaled 85 T-34-85 and 175 T-54 tanks. A subsequent arms deal in 1966 marked the first sales of the newer T-55 tank. Arms sales continued after the 1968 coup that put the Ba'ath Party in power. Moscow gave permission for the sale of its most modern export tank, the T-62, and the first 60 were delivered in 1972. By 1977, medium tank sales had totaled 867 T-54/-55s and 690 T-62s, as well as 32 PT-76 amphibious tanks. Moscow agreed to the sales of the T-72M tank and the first arrived in 1979, initially equipping the 17th Armored Brigade in Baghdad. The T-72 was the most modern Iraqi tank in the 1991 conflict.

The T-72 tank had entered production at the Uralvagonzavod plant in Nizhni-Tagil as a mobilization tank, inferior in some respects to the premier Soviet tanks, the T-64A and the later T-80. The T-72 was intended for second-echelon units deep inside the Soviet Union, while the premium tanks were forward-deployed with the Group of Soviet Forces-Germany, in the Warsaw Pact countries, and in the Soviet western military districts. The T-72 was also intended for licensed manufacture by the Warsaw Pact. In 1982, production of the T-72 in place of the T-55A began at Poland's Bumar-Łabędy plant and at Czechoslovakia's Martin plant.

The initial export model of the T-72 was internally designated as Izdeliye 172M-E, the "E" indicating Eksportniy. These were essentially similar to the original Soviet T-72, with the TPD2-49 optical rangefinder and homogenous steel turret armor. The export types were tailored to the clients. Those sold to Iraq in the first batch were Izd. 172M-E1. The "E1" variants were a special configuration for clients in the Middle East and were not fitted with the full CBR (chemical/biological/radiological) collective protective system found in Warsaw Pact tanks.

Iraq unveiled its up-armored tank, variously named the Al-Najm (*Star*) or Al-Faw, at the 1989 Baghdad military industry show. This prototype was based on a Chinese Type 69-II but many of the actual conversions were based on T-55 tanks. This configuration is popularly called the "Enigma tank" in the West. (Christopher Foss)

This was followed in 1980 by the Middle East export version T-72M (Izd. 172M-1-E4) that added a thermal sleeve to the 125mm gun, increased the ammunition stowage from 39 to 44 rounds, replaced the optical rangefinder with the TPDK-1 laser rangefinder, introduced the improved TNP-1-49-23 night sight, added the Tucha smoke grenade launchers to the front of the turret, and added the anti-HEAT[1] side skirts. Like the E1, the E4 version also lacked the full Warsaw Pact CBR protective suite.

At the time of the outbreak of the Iran–Iraq War in 1980, the Iraqi Army tank force numbered about 2,550 tanks, including 150 T-72s, 1,300 T-62s, 1,050

1   HEAT: High Explosive Anti-Tank, referring to antitank rockets and missiles using shaped-charge warheads.

Iraq's T-55QM2 was a Type 69-II tank with the 125mm gun from the T-72 substituting for the usual 100mm gun. To permit the much larger gun to fit inside the turret, Iraqi engineers elevated the two flat roof panels with an armored spacer ring. This was probably the only tank actually converted as none of these conversions were encountered during the 1991 ground campaign. (Christopher Foss)

T-54/-55s, and 50 T-34-85s. Iraq had placed large orders for the new T-72M tank prior to the war, but they had not yet been delivered. Moscow was not entirely happy with Iraq's invasion of Iran in September 1980, and imposed an arms embargo. This forced Baghdad to turn to Western countries and China for new armored vehicles. China signed a major weapons deal in 1980 for more than 2,000 tanks.

The Chinese Type 69-II eventually became the most common Iraqi tank during the Iran–Iraq War. It is worth examining in some detail since it is not as well-known as the various Soviet types used by Iraq. The Type 69 was an effort by the main Chinese tank plant, Factory No 617 in Batou, to improve the Type 59, a license-produced copy of the Soviet T-54, using features of the Soviet T-62 tank. The Chinese Army had captured a single Soviet T-62 tank during the 1969 border war. The first version, the Type 69-I (WZ-121), used a new smoothbore 100mm gun developed from the smoothbore 115mm gun of the T-62. This was not very successful and led to a decision to return to the rifled 100mm gun on the Type 69-II (WZ-121A) that became the principal production type of this tank. The Type 69-II entered production in 1978 and gave China a tank roughly comparable to the Soviet T-55. China tripled its tank production between 1980 and 1983 to accommodate Iraq's massive tank purchases.

The Type 69 introduced the new JSFCS-212 Simplified Fire Control System with a TLR1A (tank laser rangefinder) and BC1A ballistic computer. A new stabilized gunner's sight was also developed, the Type 70. The Type 69-II was also the first member of the Type 59/69 family to use active infrared night fighting equipment, as well as the first to use two-axis stabilization for the gun. The Chinese active infrared system was a copy of the Soviet Luna system, which had been in use on Soviet tanks since the early 1950s. Other additions included a CBR protection system, which had been requested by the Iraqis since they had employed chemical weapons against Iran. The Type 69 was powered by the upgraded Type 12150L-7BW diesel engine, offering 580hp at 2,000rpm. The Type 69-II

A rear view of one of the Al-Faw/Al-Najm Enigma tanks captured by the British 1st Armoured Division in Kuwait. The large boxes behind the turret were intended to protect the rear of the turret, but they were spaced out far from the turret to provide a counterweight to the boxes fitted on the front of the turret.

can be distinguished from the earlier Type 59 family by the rear engine plate, which has a small elliptical bulge at the bottom for the cooling fan, somewhat reminiscent of the Soviet T-62. This version also has the driver's headlights mounted in two pairs on the fenders, not on the hull glacis plate as on the Type 59.

Although most of the technology on the Type 69-II was derived from Soviet tanks, the Chinese did introduce some of their own innovations. These features were introduced gradually during Chinese production from 1978–83, so Iraq ended up with a wide range of Type 69-II tanks with differing features.

One of the most distinctive Chinese innovations was turret applique armor, called "boom shields." These were a set of armored louvers mounted about 18in. from the turret sides. They were intended to disrupt the detonation of HEAT warheads, especially the RPG-7 rocket-propelled grenade. This was based on lessons from the Sino–Vietnamese War of 1979, where Chinese tank units had suffered heavy tank losses. Some Type 69-IIs only had a rear-mounted set of the grid shields vehicles have, but had a set of grid shields that fully encompassed the turret. Other innovations on the Type 69-II included an array of smoke grenade launchers on the turret and a new saw-tooth skirt shield.

This is the mysterious contents of the armored boxes of the Iraqi Enigma tank. The laminate array of alternating steel, aluminum, and rubber, with spaces between, may seem crude, but it was actually similar to the secret NERA (Non-Energetic Reactive Armor) arrays of NATO and Soviet tanks of the period. Where the Iraqis obtained this technology remains a mystery.

After a six-month arms embargo, Moscow reversed course in March 1981. Soviet leaders were dismayed to see that Iraq had responded to the Soviet embargo by signing $7 billion in arms agreements with China and other countries. As a first step to return to Baghdad's good graces, Moscow gave permission to the Warsaw Pact countries to sell tanks to Iraq. When it became clear that Moscow's hopes to curry favor with Iran had failed, Moscow resumed the delivery to Iraq of tanks that had been ordered prior to the embargo, as well as signing new tank sales agreements with Baghdad.

The two main tank producers in the Warsaw Pact, Poland and Czechoslovakia, had problems selling new tanks to Iraq since they were in the process of shifting from production of the T-55A to the new T-72. Czechoslovakia had shut down T-55A production in 1981–82, and so sold no T-55A tanks to Iraq except for some armored recovery vehicles. Czechoslovakia eventually sold Iraq 90 T-72M1 tanks, starting in 1986. On the other hand, Poland sold 690 T-55A tanks to Iraq, starting in 1981, and switched to T-72 sales in 1986. Romania reportedly sold Iraq 50 of its versions of the T-55, the TR-77, or TR-580. Several other countries sold Iraq second-hand T-54A and T-55 tanks, including North Yemen (43) and Egypt (200).

Another of the mysterious Iraqi innovations was this infrared jammer fitted to some Iraqi T-72 tanks. This was intended to interfere with the autotracker used by NATO antitank missiles such as the Milan and TOW (Tube-launched, Optically tracked, Wire-guided) systems. The source of this device is obscure. This particular example was fitted to a Polish-manufactured T-72M1 of the 17th Armored Brigade of the RGFC Hammurabi Division captured by the US 24th Infantry Division (Mech).

Iraqi tank imports, 1981–86

Year	1981	1982	1983	1984	1985	1986	Total
Type 59			58	103			161
Type 69-II	100	460	480	630	330		2,000
T-55	468	245	101	210	25		1,049
T-62	64	57					121
T-72	156	216	91	200		282	945
PT-76		15	15				30
Total	788	993	745	1,143	355	282	4,306

Source: *CIA Handbook of Major Foreign Weapon Systems Exported to the Third World 1981–1986*

By the late 1980s, the Soviet Union had agreed to sell Iraq its best export tank, the T-72M1, in its Izd. 172M1-E6 export variant. The E6 version introduced a new turret with an enlarged frontal cavity filled with cast aluminum that provided better protection against shaped-charge warheads such as antitank missiles. It also included an additional sheet of armor on the glacis plate to defeat more modern APFSDS (Armor-Piercing, Fin-Stabilized Discarding Sabot) projectiles comparable to the Israeli M111 105mm round. The T-72M1 was otherwise very similar to the T-72M. In total, Iraq purchased 1,038 T-72s of all types, with 962 T-72 tanks still in service at the time of the 1991 conflict. The Soviet Union sold Iraq about 700 T-72 and T-72M tanks, Czechoslovakia 80 T-72Ms, and the remainder from Poland. In 1991, the T-72 was used mainly in the Republican Guard units, the main exception being the regular army's 3rd Saladin Armored Division.

Iraq approached Moscow about the local manufacture of the T-72M tank, locally dubbed Asad Babil (Lion of Babylon). Moscow handed this task over to Poland's Bumar-Łabędy plant. The process began in 1989, with Poland providing knockdown kits that were to be assembled at a factory in Taji. A T-72M tank was displayed at an international arms exhibit in Baghdad in 1989, claiming to be an Iraqi-manufactured Asad Babil tank. According to Polish officials, this was simply a Polish T-72M, since no tanks had been completed at the Taji tank plant. The factory was destroyed by air attack in 1991 before any Asad Babil tanks were finished.

An Iraqi Type 69-II, probably from the 52nd Armored Brigade, 52nd Armored Division, captured by the US 6th Marines in Kuwait. The Type 69-II can be distinguished from the T-54A by the location of the front headlights on the fenders rather than on the glacis plate, the cooling fins on the infrared searchlight, and the boom shields on the side of the turret.

Soviet clients such as Iraq were not sold tanks comparable in quality to the best Soviet tanks. The best Iraqi version of the T-72 in 1991 was the T-72M1, which was roughly equivalent to the Soviet T-72A. The T-72A was already a decade old in 1991 and not as well armored as the newer T-72B or the premium T-64B or T-80B tanks. As importantly, the Soviet Union did not export its best tank ammunition, and the Iraqi Army was relying primarily on second-rate ammunition for its T-72 tanks.

Iraq upgraded its older tanks at the Taji plant and other facilities. The most impressive design was the so-called Enigma tank, a T-55 upgraded with NERA (Non-Energetic Reactive Armor) in containers around the turret and hull. This tank was locally called the Al-Najm (Star) or Al-Faw, named after the battle during the Iran–Iraq War. The front turret containers consisted of an outer shell of 7mm steel, while the inside comprised six panels spaced 25mm apart. These panels consisted of sandwiches of aluminum, rubber, and steel. When struck by a shaped-charge warhead, the panels bent and deflected the warhead's hypersonic stream of metallic particles, degrading its penetrating power. Tests of captured examples by the Coalition found that the package was effective in defeating some smaller guided missile warheads. The source of this technology is not known, but it resembles similar NERA arrays developed in the Soviet Union, China, and elsewhere.

A less successful upgrade was the T-55QM2, a Type 69-II with a T-72's 125mm gun. To fit the gun, the turret roof panels had to be elevated. The interior of the T-55/Type 69-II was not very spacious to begin with, and became impossibly cramped when fitted with the 125mm gun. The T-55QM2 shown at the 1989 Baghdad arms show was probably the only such conversion undertaken.

Besides these conversion efforts, Iraq also introduced infrared ATGM (Antitank Guided Missile) jammers on some of its tanks. At least two

IRAQI TYPE 69-II AND T-55 TANKS

1. Type 69-II, Iraqi 2-41st Armored Brigade, 51st Mechanized Division, February 1991. This tank was in the usual Iraqi dull sand color with a sprayed camouflage pattern of dull dark green. The side skirts are in bare metal, the searchlight in dark green, and the canvas mantlet cover in a faded gray/green. The divisional insignia was a bisected rectangle, black on the left and white on the right. Inside the right portion was a bisected triangle, with the colors indicating the regiment within the brigade as shown in the inset illustrations. In the case of this particular tank, the gray/black triangle colors are reversed from the standard pattern as shown on the inset drawing. The tank tactical number indicated company (first number), platoon (second number), and tank (letter on the left). This tank is marked 13B, and the sequence in this platoon would be 13, 13A, and 13B.

2. T-55AM, 37th Armored Brigade, Iraqi 12th Armored Division, battle of Medina Ridge, February 1991. This T-55 is finished in the usual overall dull sand color. The 12th "Nu'man ibn al-Mundhir" Division used a simple spinning triangle for its three armored brigades, painted in red and either black or dark blue. The triangle pointed to nine o'clock for the 37th, to seven o'clock for the 46th, and to 12 o'clock for the 50th Armored Brigade. Some tanks in this brigade lacked this triangle insignia. The tank tactical numbers were in black on a white rectangle, in this case 11B.

Another view of a Type 69-II captured by the 6th Marines. This rear view shows one of the distinctive features of the Type 69-II compared to the T-54A, the semicircular dip in the rear armor panel, similar to that on the T-62. This was necessitated due to the use of a larger cooling fan.

This is one of the early export models of the T-72 (Izd. 172M-E1) sold to Iraq in the late 1970s and early 1980s. It can be most easily identified by the protrusion of the TPD2-49 optical rangefinder in front of the commander's cupola, as well as the absence of a thermal sleeve on the 125mm gun. This example served with the 3rd Saladin Armored Division in the vicinity of Kuwait City.

different types were issued. These emitted an infrared beam that was intended to mimic the infrared flare on the rear of many wire-guided antitank missiles. If the autotracker on the missile launcher was fooled by the signal, it would lose track of the missile, causing it to miss its intended target. It is unclear whether this device was at all effective since the threat of such devices was well known before the 1991 war. Many ATGMs were modified to use a coded infrared signal to prevent such jamming. Another mystery is the origin of these devices, whether they were actually developed and manufactured in Iraq or purchased from an unknown country abroad.

Iraq made many other upgrades to its tanks, most notably adopting Chinese-style saw-tooth skirts on the side of their Soviet tanks and fitting the active IR searchlights with armored covers to reduce their vulnerability to artillery fragments.

Iraqi tank strength at the start of the 1991 war is not certain. Some Coalition sources estimated that the Iraqi Army had as many as 5,800–7,000 tanks in the Kuwait Theater of Operations (KTO) at the beginning of the conflict, but later assessments lowered this to the 3,475–4,300 range. Part of the problem was whether mechanically exhausted and battle-damaged tanks were counted. Iraq had captured about 600 M47s, M60A1s, Chieftains, and other tanks from Iran, though many of these were not operational. In October 1990, the Iraqi Army chief-of-staff ordered that 500 deactivated or inoperative tanks be sent to Kuwait to serve as decoys against the Coalition air attacks, further confusing the issue of how many Iraqi tanks were operational in Kuwait. Russian accounts, possibly based on Iraqi records, put overall Iraq tank strength in 1991 at 5,300, of which 3,700 were in the KTO.

US tanks

The predominant Coalition tank during the Gulf War was the M1A1 Abrams. A total of about 2,300 Abrams tanks were deployed to the KTO, of which 538 were located in operational-ready float status and theater war reserve stock. A total of 235 M1s, 1,178 M1A1s, and 594 M1A1(HA)s served with the US Army, along with 16 M1A1s and 60 M1A1(HA)s with the Marines.

The first M1 Abrams tanks to arrive in the KTO were mostly the original M1 tank, armed with the 105mm gun. This had the first generation of special armor, codenamed Green Grape. A vigorous effort was made to replace these through the fall and winter of 1990 since they were inferior in firepower and protection to the newer M1A1. By the time of the February 1991 ground campaign, only two battalions still had the old M1, the 3-37 and 4-37 Armor with the 2nd Brigade, 1st Infantry Division (Mech).

"Penetrator," an M1A1 Abrams tank of the 2nd Armored Cavalry Regiment, along the Iraqi frontier on February 12, 1991, before the start of the ground campaign.

The predominant version of the Abrams in service was the M1A1 in its several sub-variants. This version was fitted with an evolved second-generation version of the Green Grape special armor and was armed with the new 120mm gun. The first production tanks were delivered in August 1985. Priority for the new tank went to the US Army Europe (USAREUR), which began receiving them in large numbers by 1988. In October 1988, a third generation of special armor was introduced on the M1A1 that incorporated depleted uranium in its structure. This is a metallic uranium consisting of isotopes that emit little or no radiation. The principal advantage of uranium is its weight and density, about double that of lead per volume. The variant incorporating the third-generation special armor was dubbed the M1A1 HA (HA = heavy armor). In the autumn of 1990, the US Army began retrofitting the heavy armor package and other upgrades into older M1A1 tanks that had already been delivered to the KTO. These upgrades never received an official designation but are sometimes referred to as M1A1 (Mod).

M1 Abrams Tank Battalions, Operation *Desert Storm*

	M1	M1A1	M1A1 (Mod)	M1A1HA	M1A1 Common	Total
1st Armored Division		3	2	1		6
3rd Armored Division		3		3		6
1st Cavalry Division			4			4
1st Infantry Division	2		2	2		6
24th Infantry Division			4			4
Tiger Brigade (2nd Armored Division)			2			2
2nd Armored Cavalry Regiment				3*		3
3rd Armored Cavalry Regiment				3*		3
US Marine Corps				1	1**	2
Total	2	6	14	13	1	36

* Armored Cavalry Regiments were organized with three squadrons, with 41 M1A1HAs each

** Only two companies

"Damn Yankee," a M551A1(TTS) of D Company, 3-73 Armor, 82nd Airborne Division, with the various upgrades applied to the Sheridan prior to the start of the ground campaign.

The first US tanks to arrive in Saudi Arabia in 1990 were the M551A1 Sheridans of the 3-73 Armor, supporting the 82nd Airborne Division. These were upgraded prior to the ground campaign, including the addition of the Tank Thermal Sight (TTS). There were 57 in service in 1991. Some M60A3 tanks arrived with US Army units in 1990, but they were replaced with M1A1 tanks prior to the ground conflict. Records indicate that there were still nine M60A3s in Army hands when the ground war began in February 1991, but they apparently saw no use in the campaign.

The US Marine Corps depended primarily on the M60A1 RISE (Passive) tank, amounting to 277 of the 353 tanks deployed. This designation referred

US ARMY M1A1 TANKS

1. M1A1, Task Force 2-70 Armor, 1st Armored Division, battle of Medina Ridge, February 27, 1991.

This illustration shows "Bandit," the command tank of Capt Mark Gerges from 2-70 Armor. US tactical vehicles during *Desert Storm* were painted in CARC 686 (FS 33446) Tan. This was a special Chemical-Agent Resistant Coating designed to be decontaminated in the event of a chemical weapons attack without degrading the paint, as would occur with normal paints.

US Army units with the VII Corps in Germany before the Gulf War had been adopting a set of tactical markings to identify tanks. This consisted of a metal plate mounted in the tank rear bustle rack. The octagon seen in the inset indicated the 2nd Battalion. Many tanks mounted 40mm ammunition boxes for added stowage on the bustle rack, and in this case, three of the boxes were painted in bright red paint.

Most tank units during Operation *Desert Storm* applied tactical numbers on the side for quick identification of units. The basic marking was a two-digit tactical number in the center to identify tanks within a company. This number was also used with the usual bumper code on the front and rear of the tank in small letters. The number 66 indicated the company commander, 65 the executive officer, and then 11–14 for 1st Platoon, 21–24 for 2nd Platoon, etc. Around the tactical number on the hull side was a "Spinning Vee," with A Company identified with a V pointing to 12 o'clock, B Company to three o'clock, C Company to six o'clock, and D Company to nine o'clock; the HQ used two Vees, as seen here.

2. M1A1, B Company, 4-8th Cavalry, 3rd Armored Division, battle of 73 Easting, February 27, 1991. "Beowulf" shows a variation of the "Spinning Vee" tactical insignia within the 3rd Armored Division. Units in the division's 2nd Brigade often painted the tactical marking in CARC Tan on a black rectangle, as seen here. Some tanks also had the division's "Spearhead" insignia stenciled on the side.

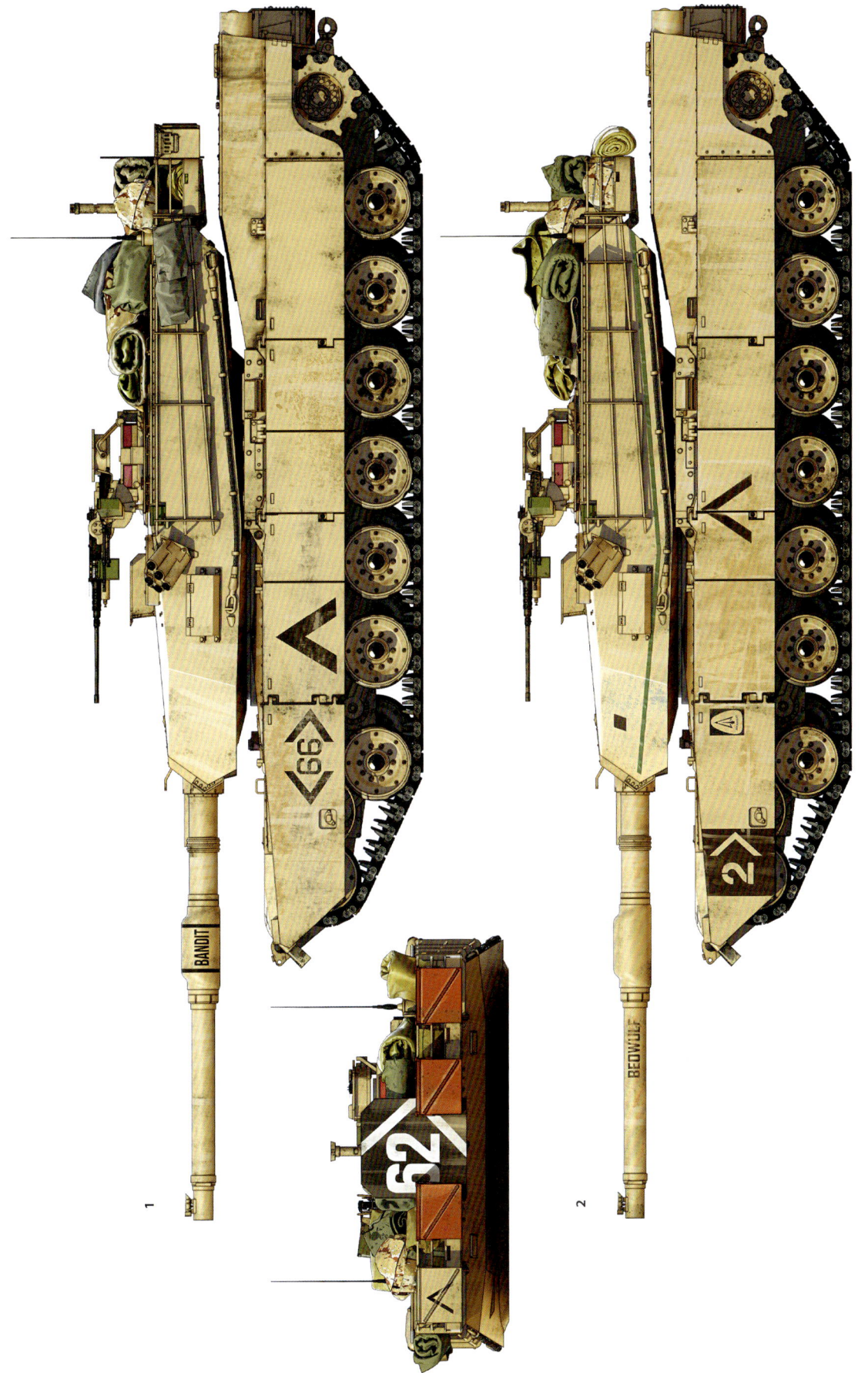

to the use of the Reliability Improved Selected Equipment package, introduced in 1975, and the passive image-intensification night viewing sights that replaced the previous active infrared system starting in 1977. Production of the M60A1 RISE (Passive) ended in 1980 in favor of the M60A3 that introduced the thermal imaging tank sight (TTS) in place of the image-intensification sight. The Marines decided against adopting this tank in favor of waiting for the arrival of the M1 Abrams later in the 1980s.

In the mid-1980s, the US Army completed the development of an explosive reactive armor kit for the M60 tank called Applique Armor, consisting of 52 M1 and 43 M2 armor tiles. The Marines decided to upgrade their M60A1 RISE (Passive) tanks with this feature after they had been delivered to the KTO.

In 1990, the Marines were still awaiting delivery of the M1A1 Common, a modified version of the M1A1 intended to unify Army/Marine requirements by incorporating some necessary Marine features such as deep wading adapters needed for amphibious operations. Efforts were made to accelerate delivery of the M1A1 tanks in early 1991. The Marine 2nd Tank Battalion was equipped with the M1A1HA, borrowed from the Army, while the two companies of the Marine Reserve 4th Tank Battalion had the new M1A1 Common tank. In total, the USMC deployed 76 M1A1 tanks in Operation *Desert Storm*, consisting of 60 M1A1HA and 16 M1A1 Common tanks.

Coalition tanks: the European Allies

The principal British tank in Operation *Granby* was the Challenger Mk. 3. A total of 226 Challenger Mk. 3 tanks were deployed to the KTO, representing about a half of total Challenger production. Of these, 174 were deployed with the three armoured regiments, the remainder were replacement tanks. On arriving in theater, the Challengers were modified to improve performance in desert conditions. Initially, it was expected that the British tank regiments would participate in the US Marine attack towards Kuwait City. In view of the likely involvement in intense urban combat, the British Army embarked on an armor upgrade effort to improve the Challenger's protection. Other improvements included the addition of disposable fuel drums on the hull rear

A Scorpion CVR(T) used by the Recce Troop of the Royal Scots Dragoon Guards, 7th Armoured Brigade.

and a smoke generation system. Firepower improvements included the debut of the new L26A1 APFSDS round, codenamed Jericho, that used a depleted uranium penetrator.

The Challenger was supported by reconnaissance vehicles of the Combat Vehicle Reconnaissance-Tracked CVR(T) family. The two principal tank types used in the conflict were the Scorpion, armed with a low-velocity 76mm gun, and the Scimitar, armed with a 30mm autocannon. About a dozen of the older Centurion tanks also saw service in the campaign in the combat engineer derivative, the Centurion AVRE.

The principal French tank in Operation *Daguet* was the AMX30B2. This was the

latest version of the AMX30 family, incorporating powerplant upgrades as well as the COTAC fire control system. The first AMX30B2 tanks were delivered in 1981, followed by several subsequent batches based on rebuilt AMX30B tanks. The late-production AMX30B2 had the DIVT16 thermal imaging sensor in place of the mid-production image intensification sight, and all Daguet tanks had this feature. Other upgrades on the Daguet tanks were the addition of Gallix smoke dischargers, sand skirts, and the LIR30 infrared decoy system. In total, 44 AMX30B2 tanks served with the 4e Régiment de Dragons in the 1991 fighting.

A Challenger I Mk 3 tank of the Royal Scots Dragoon Guards, 7th Armoured Brigade, alongside the Basra–Kuwait Highway following the retreat of the Iraqi Army in late February 1991.

Coalition tanks: the Arab forces

The Coalition Forces under the Joint Forces Command are much more poorly documented than those under CENTCOM. Details regarding the specific units involved and the numbers of tanks deployed are not generally available.

Numerically, the most significant tank in the Joint Forces Command was the M60 tank, principally the M60A1 and M60A3. Saudi Arabia had acquired 158 M60A1(RISE) tanks from 1977–79, followed by 100 M60A3(TTS) versions in 1984 and 1985. Egypt began buying the M60A3 (Passive) in 1980, and by 1989, 753 tanks had been delivered. Most of these

The M-84AB tanks of the Kuwaiti 35th Armored Brigade could be distinguished from other T-72M variants by their distinctive Yugoslav features, such as the vertical post for the meteorological sensor immediately behind the gun mantlet, the gunner's DNNS-2 day/night sight, and the additional radio antenna mounts on the roof. Note also the Coalition three white stripes on the side skirts.

were M60A3 (Passive) with image intensification sights, except for the third contract batch, which included 128 M60A3(TTS) versions with tank thermal sights. A sixth contract brought the total to 849 M60A3s, but it is not clear how many of these had been delivered prior to the Gulf War. The M60A3 served with the Egyptian 4th Armored Division that took part in the 1991 war. Bahrain purchased 54 M60A3 tanks in 1985, with deliveries taking place from 1987–88.

The next most common tank in the Joint Forces Command was the

French AMX30. Saudi Arabia was one of the first export countries for this tank, purchasing 290 examples of the modified AMX30S in 1970, with deliveries starting in 1975. This sale encouraged further export to other Gulf States, and the UAE bought 64 AMX30B tanks, starting in 1972. Qatar acquired 24 AMX30 tanks from 1977.

Kuwait had an unusual mix of tanks in 1990–91. It purchased 70 Vickers MBT Mk 1s between 1970 and 1972, and these served with the 6th Mechanized Brigade in northern Kuwait. This was followed by an order for 153 Chieftain Mk 5/2s in 1976, and these served mainly with the 35th Shaheed Armored Brigade. A small order for 24 M48A5 tanks was placed in the early 1980s, with deliveries in 1983 and 1984. Kuwait decided to replace the Chieftain with the Yugoslav M-84AB, with a contract for 200 tanks in 1989. Although the Kuwaiti Army liked the Chieftain's powerful gun, the engine was a constant source of problems. The M-84AB was a license-built version of the T-72 tank, but with local Yugoslav changes to the fire control system. During the Iraqi invasion of Kuwait on August 2, 1990, the 35th Brigade established a defensive position near Mutla Ridge, between the Al-Salem air base and the town of Jahra, eventually clashing with the RGFC Hammurabi Division in the "battle of the Bridges." Although it inflicted significant losses on the Iraqi forces, the brigade was eventually forced to withdraw into Saudi Arabia. At the time, it still had 37 Chieftain tanks. Iraq captured the remaining Kuwaiti tank arsenal, but it is unclear how many of these tanks were still operational. Deliveries of the Yugoslav M-84AB took place in the fall and winter of 1990–91 in Saudi Arabia, 're-equipping'. the Kuwaiti 35th Brigade.

Syria deployed its 9th Armored Division to Saudi Arabia and it was subordinate to the JFC-North. This division was presumably equipped with T-55 and T-62 tanks. It was held as the JFC-North reserve and saw no combat in the 1991 war.

THE CAMPAIGN

The "Mother of all Battles" began at 0200hrs on January 17, 1991, with Coalition air attacks against radars on the approaches to Baghdad. This started a month-long air campaign to degrade Iraqi defenses before the beginning of the ground campaign. The initial phase of the Coalition air strikes targeted the Iraqi air defense network, air force, and strategic targets within central Iraq.

The battle of Khafji

On the night of January 29, the Iraqi Army began a limited offensive to disrupt Coalition preparations for the ground campaign. A raid was staged by the Iraqi IV Corps in western Kuwait to distract from the main mission by III Corps to capture the coastal port of Ras al-Khafji. The 6th Brigade of the Iraqi 3rd Armored Division began its diversionary raid from the al-Wafra plantation westward into Saudi Arabia, near the old Saudi border post at al-Safra, around 2200hrs. This attack ran into a thin screen of US Marine light armored infantry companies and reconnaissance platoons of the 1st Marine Division on LAV-25 armored vehicles. The Marines held back the Iraqi force long enough for A-10 and AV-8B attack aircraft to arrive. The 6th

The Qatari tank battalion in Saudi Arabia dispatched two companies of AMX-30B tanks to support the 7th Battalion of the Saudi Arabian National Guard's 2nd Brigade during the fighting for Khafji on January 30, 1991. They knocked out four Iraqi T-55 tanks, but lost two of their own. (Patrick Durand/Sygma via Getty Images)

Armored Brigade lost 22 tanks and AFVs, mainly to air attack, and withdrew back into Kuwait after dawn. At the same time, the Iraqi 34th Armored Brigade and 27th Mechanized Brigade of the 1st Mechanized Division staged a similar raid further north, from the vicinity of the Ahmed al-Jaber air base westwards. This attack was less vigorous, and after the Iraqi columns were halted by the Marine LAVs, the Iraqi armored vehicles were pummeled by air attack.

The main mission by the Iraqi III Corps was aimed at seizing the port of al-Khafji using elements of the 5th Mechanized Infantry Division, supported by the 3rd Armored Division. The spearhead of the attack, the 26th Armored Brigade of the 5th Mechanized Division, began pushing down the coast road at 2015hrs to clear a path for the 15th and 20th Mechanized Brigades. The immediate tactical goal was to seize al-Khafji before daylight and to establish strong defensive positions around the town. There were no Coalition defenses in the town except for outposts, and the civilian population had

A column from Task Force Breach Alpha, 2nd Marine Division, is led by a M60A1 RISE (Passive Applique Armor) fitted with Track Width Mine Plough (TWMP) to assist in breaching the forward Iraqi minefields. It is followed by a column of AAV-7PA1 amtracs. The orange panel on the rear turret roof is an air identification panel.

been evacuated the previous August at the time of Iraq's invasion of Kuwait. The Iraqi attack proceeded against no resistance, and the port was in Iraqi hands by 0200hrs on January 30.

The first Coalition attacks were conducted after dawn by Marine AH-1W Super Cobra attack helicopters firing TOW (Tube-launched, Optically tracked, Wire-guided) antitank missiles. The Saudi government was infuriated by the Iraqi capture of Saudi territory, and JFC-East was tasked with destroying the Iraqi invasion force as quickly as possible before Saddam turned it into a propaganda victory. The JFC-East forces in the immediate vicinity were two battalions of the 2nd Saudi National Guard Brigade, an M60A1 tank company of the 8th Ministry of Defense and Aviation (MODA) Brigade, and elements of the Qatari Brigade with AMX30 tanks. JFC-East deployed the 5-2nd SANG Brigade and the 8th MODA Brigade to the north of Khafji to block the road, while the 7-2nd SANG Brigade and the Qatari Brigade approached Khafji from the southwest. The first tank skirmishes began when Qatari AMX30 tanks engaged several T-55 tanks in the outskirts of the town on the morning of January 30. US forces provided artillery and air support, directed by forward observers in the town and at nearby outposts. The US air attacks were focused on the Kuwaiti side of the border to prevent Iraqi reinforcement of Khafji.

The main Saudi ground attack began around 2000hrs on January 30, by the 7th Battalion, 2nd SANG Brigade, supported by two companies of Qatari AMX30 tanks. The Saudi battalion was mounted on Cadillac Gage V-150 wheeled APCs and made a cavalry charge directly into the town. After intense close-quarter fighting, the battered 7th Battalion was withdrawn to recuperate on the afternoon of January 31. The effort then shifted to the 8th Battalion, 2nd SANG Brigade. Khafji was captured by February 1, though clean-up operations in the town continued for a few days. The Iraqis lost over 90 tanks and AFVs, while JFC-East lost ten Saudi V-150 AFVs and two Qatari AMX30 tanks.

While Khafji was not the largest battle of the Gulf War, it was one of the most consequential. Prior to Khafji, Coalition analysts were divided in their assessments of the combat effectiveness of the Iraqi Army. Some portrayed the Iraqi Army as a well-equipped, battle-hardened, determined foe. Khafji and the associated raids suggested otherwise. A later assessment concluded that "Khafji showed [the Iraqis] as incapable at this stage of the war of mounting an operational maneuver involving multiple divisions."

D

COALITION TANKS

1. Challenger 1 Mk 3, Royal Scots Dragoon Guards, 4th Troop, A Squadron, 7th Armoured Brigade, Operation *Granby*. Challengers in Operation *Granby* were painted in BS381C-361 Light Stone. The call sign "40" indicates the 4 Troop leader. The usual Coalition "∧" is painted on the side. On the roof is a TOGS indicator intended to permit neighboring tanks to identify the troop from any angle. It consisted of two sheets of metal perpendicular to one another in a diamond shape attached to a metal post. In this fashion, the shape was visible from anywhere. Other troops used circles, diamonds, and rectangles. A small Scottish flag is painted on the side of the TOGS housing.

2. AMX-30B2, 4e Règiment de Dragons, 6e Division Légère Blindée, Operation *Daguet*. The tanks during Operation *Daguet* were painted in the "Zone Outre-Mer" (Overseas Area) scheme consisting of two-thirds *Sable désert IR* (Desert sand infrared) and one-third in *Brun terre IR* (Earth brown infrared). The infrared in the paint name refers to the paint's infrared suppression features. There are two of the Coalition "∧" markings on the side, with a small dot in the upper right. The tank tactical number was carried on the forward sand skirt, in this case indicating 1e escadron, 1e peleton, 2e engin (1st Squadron, 1st Platoon, 2nd Vehicle).

The air campaign intensifies

At the end of January 1991, the air campaign against Iraq began to put more focus on degrading the forward-deployed Iraqi units in the Kuwaiti Theater of Operations KTO. Initial strikes using unguided "dumb" bombs were not particularly effective, since nothing short of a direct hit could destroy a tank. On February 8, the F-111 crews began using "tank plinking" tactics, dropping laser-guided GBU-12 500lb bombs. This proved very successful and the tactic was emulated by A-6E Intruders and F-15E Strike Eagles. The other effective anti-armor weapon was the AGM-65 Maverick guided missile, fired from A-10, F-16, F/A-18, and AV-8B aircraft. A total of 5,255 Mavericks were launched, 4,801 from A-10 aircraft, with an estimated hit rate of 80 percent.

The amount of destruction of Iraqi tanks varied from unit to unit. Units near the frontier were subjected to especially intense attacks. The VII Corps commander, Gen Frederick Franks, singled out the Iraqi 52nd Armored Brigade because it was positioned on the corps' exposed right flank. Franks told the joint targeting team to make the 52nd "go away," so it became known as the "Go-Away Brigade." Air attacks began on January 17 and continued until the start of the ground campaign. By this time, the brigade had been reduced to about 10 percent of its original tank and AFV strength, even after having received replacement vehicles.

The actual number of tanks and AFVs destroyed by air attack was controversial, with some ground commanders later arguing that the air forces had exaggerated their claims. This is detailed below in the Battle Analysis section. Nonetheless, the air attacks thoroughly demoralized the Iraqi troops, particularly those in the forward infantry divisions that suffered the brunt of the air attacks. One consequence of the attacks was that Iraqi tank crews did not regularly man their tanks, but instead would live in dugouts positioned a hundred yards away from the tanks. As a result, during the ensuing ground campaign, Coalition tank units often surprised Iraqi tank forces and destroyed many tanks before their crews could get back to them.

The Iraqi response to the air attacks was largely ineffective, since the forward-deployed regular army units lacked sufficient radar-directed guns and missiles. The Republican Guard divisions deeper in Kuwait had better

"Skeezer Pleazer," a M1A1 of C Company, 2nd Marine Tank Battalion, fitted with a Track Width Mine Plow during the advance into Kuwait during the ground campaign. The tank name probably refers to the 1986 album by the American musical group UTFO.

An Iraqi T-55 of the 2nd Armored Regiment, 12th Armored Brigade, 3rd Saladin Armored Division, knocked out along the "Highway of Death" near the Mutla Pass west of Kuwait City during the fighting with the Tiger Brigade.

weapons, so attacks against them required more complicated tactics. The Iraqis attempted several passive defense techniques. Project Tariq was an effort to ignite oil fires in front of the troops in the hope that the resulting smoke would degrade visibility enough to thwart precision air attacks. Even the Iraqis admitted that this scheme had only limited value.

By G-Day, the start of the ground campaign on February 24, CENTCOM estimated that the combat effectiveness of the forward Iraqi divisions had been reduced to 50 percent due to casualties, desertion, lack of supplies, and disruption on the command-and-control network. On the eve of G-Day, CENTCOM estimated that about 38 percent of Iraqi tanks and AFVs had been knocked out, as is detailed in the accompanying table.

Degradation of Iraqi armored strength in KTO (Cumulative Losses)

Date	Tanks	APC/IFV
Jan 22	14	0
Jan 27	65	50
Feb 1	476	243
Feb 6	728	552
Feb 11	862	692
Feb 16	1,439	879
Feb 21	1,563	887
Feb 23	1,688	929
Feb 24	1,772	948
Original strength	4,280	2,880

G-Day

The start of the ground campaign began in the pre-daylight hours of G-Day – Sunday, February 24, 1991. The weather was overcast and rainy, with visibility further reduced by the oil fires ignited by the Iraqis. The Coalition ground forces were organized into three principal commands: Joint Forces Command in the east, attacking into Kuwait; VII Corps, attacking into the desert immediately west of the Iraq–Kuwaiti border; and XVIII Airborne Corps, forming a covering force on the extreme western side of the Coalition advance.

The Joint Forces Command attack

The Joint Forces Command's immediate task was to overcome the fortified Iraqi defenses along the southern Kuwaiti border. JFC-East was oriented towards the southeastern sector, with a focus on the road to Kuwait City, while the I Marine Expeditionary Force attacked in the center around the "elbow" of the Saudi–Kuwait border, and JFC-West was assigned to advance along the western Iraq–Kuwaiti border. The brunt of the initial attack was borne by the I Marine Expeditionary Force with JFC-North largely immobile for the first two days of the fighting.

The initial stage of the Marine attack involved breaching the layered Iraqi defenses, which included barbed wire obstacles, minefields, fire trenches,

A T-72M of the Iraqi 3rd Saladin Armored Division knocked out near Ali al-Salam airbase west of Kuwait City during the fighting with the Tiger Brigade. It is fitted with the mount for an ATGM (Antitank Guided Missile) jammer on the turret side, though the jammer itself isn't evident in this photo. A penetration by an APFSDS (Armor-Piercing, Fin-Stabilized Discarding Sabot) round can be seen on the rear side of the turret. This tank has suffered a catastrophic ammunition fire that lifted the turret off the hull and collapsed the torsion bar suspension.

E **IRAQI T-62 TANKS**

1. T-62 M1970, Armored Regiment, 25th Mechanized Brigade, Iraqi 6th Armored Division. This T-62 is finished in the usual Iraqi dull sand color. The 6th Armored Division had the usual type of divided geometric insignia to distinguish subunits. The 12th Armored Brigade used red/white, the 25th Mechanized Brigade red/grey, and the 30th Armored Brigade red/yellow. The colored band on the right of the insignia indicated the regiment within the brigade, in this case a black band for the armored regiment. This particular tank had its army license plate attached to the front of the turret instead of in the usual position on the center of the lower lip of the glacis plate or on the hull rear. The green license plate usually had the Iraqi armed forces triangle at the right or left of the plate with a five-digit registration number, in this case 10081. Iraqi tanks often used ordinary commercial 55-gallon fuel drums, which appeared in various commercial colors such as dull red or blue.

2. T-62 M1970, 3rd Armored Regiment, 6th Armored Brigade, 3rd Saladin Armored Division, February 1991. The Iraqi 3rd Armored Division based their tactical markings on a grey circle with an internal rectangle. The basic color of the rectangle was white for the 6th Armored Brigade and black for the 12th Armored Brigade. The color of the square in the center of the rectangle indicated the regiment. Above the rectangle in Arabic was "QX," for Qādisiyyah Xaddam. Al-Qādisiyyah was the location of a famous battle in AD 636, and "Saddam's Qādisiyyah" was an alternative for the slogan "Mother of all Battles," suggesting that the 1991 conflict would be a great victory like the battle of Qādisiyyah. The tank regiments of the 3rd Armored Division also painted the fume extractors on the gun barrel in chrome yellow with a white stripe. This tank is number 11A.

1

2

berms, and prepared defenses. The Marines began by infiltrating the initial barriers shortly after midnight. Minefields were breached using rocket-propelled line charges, followed by tanks with mine plows. A typical breaching force was the Marine 2nd Division's Task Force Breach Alpha that consisted of 18 AAV-7A1 amtracs – each with M154 three-shot mine-clearing line-charges – two M60A1 dozer tanks, 16 M60A1 tanks with track-width mine plows towing a M59 line-charge trailer, four M60A1 tanks with mine rakes, six M1A1 tanks with mine plows, 22 AAVP-7A1s with engineer squads, 15 M9 armored combat earthmovers, and 39 M58 line-charge trailers. The cleared lanes were marked by engineers and the task forces continued to grind through successive obstacle belts. The breaching units suffered the most casualties on G-Day, with the Marine 2nd Division suffering mine damage to seven M60A1 tanks, one M1A1 tank, and two AAV-7A1 amtracs.

Iraqi resistance was far less than expected, with hundreds of demoralized enemy troops surrendering at the first opportunity. In the Marine 1st Division sector, the Iraqi defense in front of al-Jaber air base collapsed. The 1st Marine Division captured or destroyed 600 tanks and 450 AFVs on the first day, along with 10,365 prisoners. The Marine 2nd Division captured the Iraqi 9th Tank Battalion intact, along with its 35 T-55 tanks.

The I MEF met its first serious resistance on G+1, February 25. The commander of the Iraqi III Corps, General Salah Aboud, ordered a pincer attack, consisting of the 7th Infantry Division attacking from the north and the 5th Mechanized Division attacking from the al-Burqan oil field. The Iraqi 8th Infantry Division and 3rd Armored Division were to reinforce the attack from the northeast. Around dawn, elements of the Iraqi 22nd Armored Brigade, 5th Mechanized Division, emerged out of the early-morning fog and smoke and began attacking the 1st Marine Division. A mixed force

An Egyptian Army M60A1 on exercise with M1A1 tanks of the 24th Infantry Division (Mech) after the Gulf War. The red triangle marking identifies it as being from a division of the Second Field Army.

of Iraqi tanks and APCs approached the Marine 1st Division headquarters, but were beaten off by M60A1 tanks of the Marine 3rd Tank Battalion. As the fog gradually lifted, the Marine 1st Tank Battalion engaged in a confused fight with the remainder of the Iraqi brigade, gaining control of the battlefield by 1100hrs. The Iraqis lost most of two brigades during the morning attacks, including 50 tanks and 25 APCs.

In the neighboring sector, the Marine 2nd Division was hit by the "Reveille Counterattack" around 0620 from the Iraqi 7th Infantry Division and 3rd Armored Division. Company B, Marine 4th Tank Battalion equipped with M1A1 tanks, was north of Al Jaber air base when they spotted a column of new Iraqi T-72 tanks of the 3rd Armored Division passing through a formation of T-55 tanks in revetments. The poor visibility blinded the Iraqi tanks, but the Marine M1A1 tanks were able to use their thermal sights to peer through the gloom. In a matter of minutes, 34 of 35 tanks were knocked out.

An M-84AB tank of the Kuwaiti 35th Ash-Shahid (*Martyr's*) Armoured Brigade during operations in Kuwait at the conclusion of the fighting. The brigade lost two tanks in combat during the conflict, though they were later recovered.

By the afternoon of February 25, the Iraqi III Corps had been pushed back to the outskirts of Kuwait City, with the Marine 1st Division on their heels. The III Corps commander reported to Baghdad that three of his infantry divisions were combat ineffective and that he was taking steps to defend the city with the surviving forces. Shortly after, Baghdad ordered the III Corps to withdraw towards Basra, effectively abandoning Kuwait. The hasty retreat was spotted by Coalition forces, and relentless air attacks on the roads leading out of Kuwait City created the "Highway of Death" west of the city.

The Marine 1st Division continued to encounter resistance from remnants of Iraqi forces in the al-Burqan oil fields, with an intense armored confrontation occurring after dark on February 25. Around 2200hrs, the Marine 1st Division was ordered to proceed and seize Kuwait City airport. The fighting around the airport continued for most of February 26.

On the I MEF's left flank, the M1A1 tanks of Tiger Brigade began a rapid advance towards Mutla Ridge to the west of Kuwait City, along the seam of the Iraqi III and IV corps. This was intended to cut off any Iraqi retreat out of Kuwait City not already caught up in the "Highway of Death." The Tiger Brigade encountered and destroyed numerous Iraqi tank detachments in revetments on the approaches to the suburb of Al Jahrah. During the four days of fighting, Tiger Brigade destroyed or captured 181 Iraqi tanks and 148 APCs, mostly on February 26 and 27.

By agreement with Joint Forces Command, on February 27, Saudi and Egyptian units of JFC-North and JFC-East wheeled north of the I MEF lines in order to liberate Kuwait City. The Egyptian 3rd Mechanized Division and 4th Armored Division secured positions to the northwest of Al Jahrah, and the Saudi 20th Armored Division to the southwest. On the Gulf side, Saudi units from JFC-East entered Kuwait City from the south. During the four days of fighting, the Marines had destroyed 460 tanks and captured another 600, destroyed 218 APCs and captured a further 390, and captured 22,308 Iraqi troops.

An Iraqi T-55 tank, probably from the tank battalion of the 49th Infantry Division, knocked out at Jalibah airfield on February 27, 1991, during combat with the 2nd Vanguard Brigade, 24th Infantry Division (Mech).

The T-72 often suffered catastrophic ammunition fires, with a resulting explosion that threw its turret in the air. This is a view of a destroyed T-72M1 of the Hammurabi Division from an AH-64 Apache attack helicopter of 1-24 Aviation, 24th Infantry Division (Mech), during the March 2 fighting near the Hawr-al-Hammār waterway.

The XVIII Airborne Corps

The XVIII Airborne Corps was on the far left flank of the Coalition forces west of Kuwait in the open desert. The westernmost force, the French 6e Division Légère Blindée, reinforced by the 2nd Brigade, 82nd Airborne Division, set off into the open desert at 0100hrs on February 24. Their objective was the As Salman road junction and the nearby air base. They initially collided with the Iraqi 45th Infantry Division, which had been savagely degraded by air attacks. This division was overrun at the cost of 27 French casualties, and the French knocked out ten tanks and three BMP-1s. Behind the French, the two remaining brigades of the 82nd Airborne Division cleared the roads for future logistics requirements.

The main XVIII Airborne Corps mission was conducted by the 101st Airborne Division, with a heliborne assault 110 miles into Iraq. The mission was delayed due to weather and began around 0705hrs with 60 UH-60 and 40 CH-47 helicopters lifting the 1st Brigade into Operating Base (OB) Cobra, one of the largest heliborne operations in history. Later in the day, the 101st Airborne leapfrogged again to seize control of Highway 8, 170 miles inside Iraq.

To the east of OB Cobra, the 24th Infantry Division (Mech) began its advance at 1500hrs, with the objective of securing the Euphrates River valley to prevent the escape of Iraqi forces in Kuwait. By the end of the day, the division had advanced 75 miles into Iraq against negligible resistance.

These missions continued on February 25, with the 101st Airborne Division reaching a blocking position on the south bank of the Euphrates River near An Nasiriyah. The 24th Infantry Division advanced to its objectives against very weak opposition from elements of the Iraqi 26th and 35th Infantry Divisions, and reached the Euphrates River late in the day. The first significant Iraqi resistance was encountered on February 26 when the 24th Infantry Division fought with elements of the Iraqi 47th and 49th Infantry Divisions and the Republican Guard Nebuchadnezzar Division. The following day, the 24th Division continued to move towards Basra by taking the Tallil and Jalibah air bases, overrunning elements of the Republican Guard Hammurabi Division. During its four-day advance, the 24th Infantry Division had knocked out or captured about 360 tanks and AFVs.

The VII Corps

The most powerful element of the Coalition was the VII Corps, which advanced into the Iraqi desert to the immediate west of Kuwait. The Iraqi Army had discounted the idea that a large mechanized force could operate in these desert wastes, so the area was not heavily defended. The original plan had been to start the VII Corps offensive on G+1, February 25, but the speedy progress of the neighboring XVIII Corps led to the decision to start 14 hours early. The left wing of the advance consisted of the 1st and 3rd Armored Divisions, with the 2nd Armored Cavalry Regiment (ACR) in the lead, heading for the road junction of Al Busayyah about 80 miles from the border. Closer to the Kuwait border, the 1st Infantry Division and 1st Cavalry Division were given the task of penetrating the Iraqi border defenses, with the British 1st Armoured Division to serve as the exploitation force. The weather was "more like Germany than Arabia," in the words of one American tanker – cold, windy, rainy, and overcast. On G-Day, VII Corps' advance netted only 1,300 prisoners, a clear indication of the weak Iraqi defenses in the sector. The advance by the corps' left flank proceeded smoothly, with the US 1st Armored Division destroying about 40–50 Iraqi tanks in a violent ten-minute firefight.

An M1A1 Abrams tank of the 3rd Phantom Brigade, 1st Armored Division, during the advance into Iraq at the end of February 1991.

An Iraqi Type 69-II command tank knocked out by the US Army during the ground campaign. The command tanks can be identified by the two boxes on the rear plate. Two versions were in service: the WZ121B that had one Type 889 and one Type 892 radio, and the WZ121C that had two Type 889 radios

In front of VII Corps' right flank was the Iraqi Jihad Corps, including the 10th and 12th Armored Divisions. Late on February 24, two armored brigades of the 12th Armored Division and one from the 10th Armored Division were instructed to cover Wadi-Al-Batin along the western Kuwait border and to serve as a shield while the RGFC heavy divisions began to move towards the oncoming threat. The heaviest fighting on G+1 erupted along the corps' right flank as the US 1st Infantry Division continued the breach of the Iraqi 26th Infantry Division defensive lines in preparation for exploitation by the British 1st Armoured Division. The Iraqi VII Corps attempted to stem the advance by deploying its tactical reserve, the 52nd Armored Division. This became entangled and smashed in a one-sided night fight with British Challenger tanks late on February 25. By midnight of February 25/26, most of the Iraqi VII Corps had been routed. The British 7th Armoured Brigade was credited with the destruction of 76 tanks and 68 APCs during the fighting.

 IRAQI T-72 TANKS

1. T-72M1, 52nd Armored Regiment, 8th Armored Brigade, RFGC 1st Hammurabi Division, February 1991. The RFGC 1st Hammurabi Division used tactical markings consisting of a square with a red triangle inside. The 8th Brigade used a grey square, while the 17th Brigade used white. The colored stripe at the bottom indicated the regiment, so in the case of the 8th Brigade it was white (1st/52nd), black (2nd/53rd), and yellow (3rd/54th) Armored Brigades. This particular vehicle is number 12B. These markings were carried on the rear stowage bin and the right side stowage bin, as shown in the inset drawing; they apparently were not carried on the left side. This unit carried a large white rectangle on the side skirts, the meaning of which is not known. Likewise, there was a single white band on the barrel of undetermined purpose.

2. T-72M1, 3rd Armoured Regiment, 12th Armored Brigade, 3rd Tawakalna Armored Division, February 1991. The markings for the 12th Armored Brigade followed the same pattern as the T-62 of the 6th Armored Brigade shown in Plate E. In the case of the 12th Armored Brigade, the basic marking was a gray circle with a black rectangle. The colored square in the center of the black rectangle indicated the regiment, in this case black for the 2nd Regiment. Some of the tanks of this brigade had "Asad Babil" (*Lion of Babylon*) painted on the side skirts. This was a reference to the name given to the project to build the T-72M locally in Iraq, a program that failed to materialize. In this case, the tank number "23" is painted in white on the turret side behind the smoke mortars; often this was painted on the right side stowage bin behind the unit marking. This tank is painted with the usual yellow fume extractor with white band.

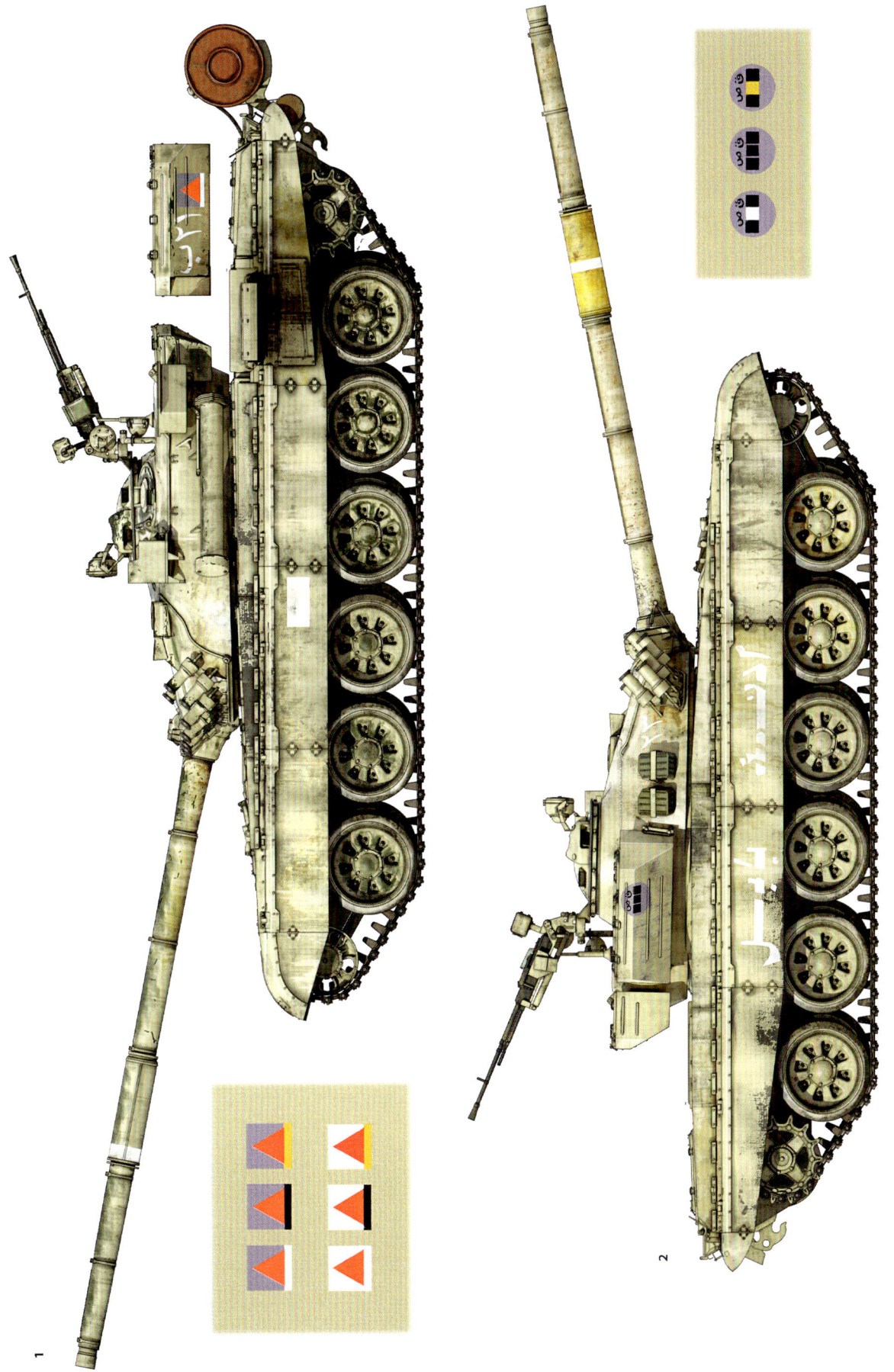

1

2

On February 26, the left flank of VII Corps overran the headquarters and logistics center of the Iraqi VII Corps and began to encounter the RGFC Tawakalna Mechanized Division. At this point, the US 1st and 3rd Armored Divisions began their planned wheeling motion to the east to strike the main concentration of Republican Guard divisions in northwestern Kuwait. Around noon, the 2nd ACR, spearheading VII Corps' left wing, started bumping into advance elements of the Iraqi 50th Brigade, 12th Armored Division, and began a one-sided engagement against a battalion of T-55 tanks and MT-LB armored transporters.

During the evening of February 25, three RGFC heavy divisions began to reorient themselves to counter the rapidly approaching VII Corps. The RGFC Tawakalna Mechanized Division deployed in a defensive blocking position on the western Kuwaiti border, with surviving elements of the 12th Armored Division to its south and the 10th Armored Division behind it to its east. The RGFC Medina and Hammurabi armored divisions were placed north on either side of the Rumaylah oil fields. The stage was set for the most intense tank fights of Operation *Desert Storm*.

At dawn on February 26, the 2nd ACR continued its advance and fought against isolated T-55 tanks and MT-LB transporters from the 12th Armored Division's remaining brigades. The intensity of the fighting convinced the 2nd ACR that it had finally entered the outer security zone of the RGFC Tawakalna Division. By mid-afternoon, the 2nd ACR as well as the neighboring 3rd Armored Division on its left encountered dug-in T-72 tanks and BMP-1 infantry fighting vehicles. Although much of the Iraqi Army was in full-scale retreat from Kuwait, the Tawakalna Division showed every sign of defending the line against the approaching VII Corps.

In the late afternoon, the 2nd ACR ran into the Iraqi 9th Armored Battalion and 18th Mechanized Battalion on the left flank of the Tawakalna Division, in prepared defensive positions to the west of the IPSA pipeline near the 73 Easting gridline. This began one of the most intense tank-vs-tank battles of the war. Two troops of the 2nd ACR fought

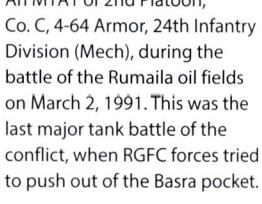

An M1A1 of 2nd Platoon, Co. C, 4-64 Armor, 24th Infantry Division (Mech), during the battle of the Rumaila oil fields on March 2, 1991. This was the last major tank battle of the conflict, when RGFC forces tried to push out of the Basra pocket.

scattered Iraqi defenses before being counterattacked by a company of T-72 tanks, which were destroyed by M1A1 tanks at 2,100m. The Iraqi position lacked an adequate security zone, so when the American vehicles arrived out of the rain and mist, they were completely unexpected. Some Iraqi crews were huddled down in trenches due to earlier air attacks in the area and never managed to get back into their vehicles. Other Iraqi tanks did fight back, but they could barely see the attacking American force and failed to properly adjust for range. The Iraqi tank fire thus

An M551A1(TTS) of 3-73 Armor, 82nd Armored Division, in Saudi Arabia prior to the start of the ground campaign. It lacks the tactical markings painted on the hull side prior to the start of the ground campaign.

hit the ground well in front of the US Army vehicles. The 18 M1A1 tanks and 24 M3A1 Bradleys destroyed more than 30 dug-in T-72 tanks and 12 BMP-1s at no loss to themselves. A captured Iraqi mechanized infantry battalion commander said that he had started the fight with 900 soldiers, a few dozen BMP-1s, and an attached battalion of 36 tanks; when he was captured, all that survived were the 40 soldiers with him. A stunned Tawakalna tank battalion commander added: "When the air campaign started, I had 39 [T-72] tanks. After 38 days of the air battle, I had 32 tanks. After 20 minutes against [the 2nd ACR], I had zero tanks." After dark, Apache helicopters struck the second tactical echelon of these brigades, causing heavy losses to three emplaced battalions.

The 3rd Armored Division hit the left flank of the Tawakalna Division in the late afternoon, pitting about eight Iraqi tank and mechanized battalions with 122 tanks and 78 BMPs against ten US heavy battalions. On the right flank of the Tawakalna Division, a tank battalion of the 29th Mechanized Brigade supported by a BMP company was overwhelmed on the evening of February 26 by the 3rd Brigade of the US 1st Armored Division. At least 24 T-72 and 14 BMP-1s were knocked out. As contact with the Tawakalna Division continued, the 1st Infantry Division passed through the overworked 2nd ACR in the dark. By midnight of G+2, after less than 30 hours of fighting, the RGFC Tawakalna Division had been destroyed bit-by-bit by the overwhelming force of three US Army heavy divisions and the 2nd ACR. Unlike most other Iraqi units, the Tawakalna Division fought tenaciously. However, its sacrifices were largely in vain due to its poor tactical skills and mediocre weapons.

On VII Corps' left flank, two brigades of the 1st Armored Division continued to move forward on the night of February 26/27, expecting to confront the RGFC Medina Armored Division on the outskirts of the Rumaila oil fields. A brigade of the RGFC Adnan Mechanized Division

G **BATTLE OF 73 EASTING, FEBRUARY 26, 1991**
The battle of 73 Easting was fought between elements of the US 2nd Armored Cavalry Regiment and the Republican Guard Tawakalna Armored Division along the 73 Easting gridline in the desert to the west of Kuwait City. The weather conditions that afternoon were poor, with frequent rain and sandstorms.

began moving into the sector to serve as a covering force, but it was spotted and shattered by US artillery fire. On the morning of February 27, the 1st Armored Division called a halt for fueling. The weather was overcast and wet, with poor visibility of only about 1,500m. The opposing 2nd Armored Brigade of the RGFC Medina Armored Division had deployed in a reverse-slope defense, but the site proved to have been poorly chosen. The US 2nd Iron Brigade of the 1st Armored Division approached the Iraqi defenses shortly after noon on February 27. The Iraqis were unaware of their approach, lacking a proper security zone and unable to see the Abrams due to the weather. The ensuing firefight was extremely one-sided. The thermal sights on the M1A1 tanks allowed the American crews to accurately locate and target the Iraqi armored vehicles while the Iraqi armored vehicles were hampered by the poor weather and mediocre tank optics. Within 15 minutes of the start of the tank duel, 37 Iraqi armored vehicles had been set on fire, many T-72 tanks exploding in gruesome fireballs, with the turrets tumbling through the air. In less than an hour of fighting on the "Medina Ridge," the 2nd Iron Brigade had knocked out 59 T-72 tanks, 29 BMP-1s, six Strela-10 air defense missile vehicles, and four other armored vehicles.

The neighboring 1st Brigade, 1st Armored Division, faced the Medina's 14th Mechanized Brigade and elements of the 46th Mechanized Brigade of the 12th Armored Division. The US Army attack began at a range of 4,000m, using thermal sights, while the Iraqis were in the process of rearming and refueling their vehicles. The Iraqi units were unprepared for the attack and generally oriented towards the south instead of facing the west, from where the attack emanated. The US 1st Armored Division's 3rd Brigade was the last to crest the ridge around 1300hrs and encountered the 2nd Mechanized Brigade of the RGFC Medina Division, which it methodically destroyed with long-range gunfire from the M1A1 tanks and TOW missile fire from the Bradleys. By the end of February 27, the 1st Armored Division had destroyed the Medina Division, knocking out 186 tanks and 127 armored infantry vehicles.

The final tank battle of the war occurred after the unilateral ceasefire declared by Coalition forces at 0800hrs on February 28. The third echelon of the Republican Guard was the Hammurabi Armored Division, which was further west behind the Rumaila oil fields. This division did not encounter US ground forces prior to the ceasefire. However, on the morning of March 2, Saddam Hussein ordered the division to escape out of the pocket because it was needed to help suppress the Shi'ite revolts against his regime that were breaking out in southern Iraq. The division attempted to escape north via an elevated causeway over the Hawr-al-Hammar waterway through a sector controlled by the US 24th Infantry Division (Mech). The column was desperate enough to fire on US Army armored vehicles, in violation of the ceasefire. The 24th Infantry Division responded by sealing off the causeway, using artillery-fired mines, then proceeded to methodically destroy the column. The 24th Division's Apache helicopters struck with 107 Hellfire missiles, scoring 102 hits, and the column was then overrun by Abrams and Bradleys, with the "battle of Rumaila" ending in the early afternoon after 187 Iraqi armored vehicles, 34 artillery pieces, and 400 trucks had been destroyed. US losses consisted of a single Abrams burned out when it was set on fire by a massive explosion from a nearby Iraqi vehicle. This was the last tank engagement of Operation *Desert Storm*.

BATTLE ANALYSIS

The 1991 Gulf War lasted only 100 hours and was the most lopsided victory in recent military history. The causes for the disastrous performance of the Iraqi Army were many, beginning with the stunning ineptitude of Saddam Hussein and the Ba'ath Party in its conduct of the war. The Iraqi Army was outclassed in all respects and suffered appallingly high losses, while inflicting minimal casualties on the Coalition forces. The average Iraqi soldier started the war with little motivation, and the Coalition air campaign led to the debilitating demoralization of most of the army except for the Republican Guard. From the US Army perspective, this was in complete contrast to the fighting spirit of adversaries such as the Chinese in the Korean War or the Vietnamese.

In terms of technical factors, the Coalition enjoyed distinct advantages in firepower and armored protection on their tanks compared to Iraqi tanks. This was most clearly the case with older Iraqi tanks such as the T-55 and Type 69-II. However, there was still a significant disparity between the best of the Iraqi tanks, the T-72M1, compared to the M1A1 Abrams or Challenger. The discrepancy between the T-72M1 and older Coalition types such as the French AMX30B2 and Marine M60A1 RISE (Passive) was not as great, but these Coalition tanks most often fought against the T-55, T-62, and Type 69-II, not the T-72.

The combat effectiveness of the T-72 tank was overrated by the US Army before the war, and many US tankers were surprised by its poor performance during the conflict. Setting aside the issue of crew quality, the T-72 suffered from several distinct technical shortcomings that became manifest in combat. The Gulf War was the first time that tank thermal sights were used extensively in combat. These were used by many of the Coalition tank forces, including the M1A1 and M551A1 of the US Army, the British Challenger, the French AMX30B2, and some Coalition M60A3(TTS) tanks. No Iraqi tank was fitted with thermal imaging sights. The main lesson from the Gulf War was not about night fighting, but rather the advantage that thermal

A knocked-out Iraqi T-62 Model 1972 of the 6th Armored Brigade, 3rd Saladin Armored Division, in a revetment on the outskirts of the Ali al-Salem air base in Kuwait. Floor tiles have been placed under the gun barrel to reduce the amount of dust kicked up when firing the main gun.

A Polish-manufactured T-55M of the Iraqi 37th Armored Brigade, 12th "Nu'man ibn al-Mundhir" Armored Division. This tank features the modified loader's hatch with the 12.7mm antiaircraft machine gun and is also fitted with a KMT-4 mine rake system.

imaging sight offered in daytime fighting. The weather conditions were almost uniformly overcast, with fog, blowing sand, and the smoke from oil fires, which resulted in poor visibility. Thermal sights were able to mitigate these conditions, as they could peer through most of the atmospheric obscurants. As a result, the M1A1 tank regularly engaged targets from ranges of 2,000m or more. In contrast, Iraqi tanks could seldom see more than 1,000m, making them essentially blind during many engagements.

The disparity in tank sight technology was not the whole story. The US Marine Corps M60A1 RISE (Passive) tanks only had image-intensification sights, which offered no advantage under the 1991 Gulf weather conditions. As a result, most Marine tank engagements took place at ranges of 1,000m or less. Nevertheless, the Marine tanks knocked out over 400 Iraqi tanks, yet did not lose any tanks to Iraqi tank fire. Clearly, the shortcomings in Iraqi crew quality were a more crippling problem than those in tank fire controls.

In terms of firepower, the Coalition tanks had a decided advantage. At the time of Operation *Desert Storm*, the preferred ammunition for the M1A1 Abrams for tank fighting was the M829A1 APFSDS round, popularly called the "Silver Bullet." Its depleted uranium penetrator had two advantages over the steel penetrator of the T-72 tank's 125mm projectile. Depleted uranium is more than twice as dense as steel, and so increased the kinetic energy on impact. Depleted uranium also offers pyrophoric effects, since its high-velocity impact against steel results in small particles that become incandescent, creating a secondary incendiary effect after penetration of the enemy tank armor, increasing internal damage to the enemy tank. Although official figures are lacking, published estimates of M829A1 penetration capabilities are 670mm at pointblank range and 570mm at 2,000m, so it was capable of penetrating the T-72M1 at normal battle ranges from any angle.

Comparative Frontal Protective Levels vs APFSD

(mm RHA)	Hull	Turret
T-72	335	380
T-72M	335	380
T-72M1	400	380
M1A1	600	600
M1A1HA	600	800

The Iraqi Army mostly used the older 3VBM-3 125mm APFSDS round in 1991, though it did have some of the improved 3VBM-7 ammunition. Both used steel penetrators. The best Soviet APFSDS at this time was the 3VBM-13 Vant with a depleted uranium penetrator that could penetrate 560mm at 2,000m, about double the performance of the 3VBM-3 used by the Iraqis; it was not available for export at the time. Although the caliber of the T-72M1's 125mm gun was larger than the M1A1's 120mm gun, the US gun offered higher chamber pressures of 5650 bar versus 4600 bar. This translated into higher projectile velocity and greater penetration power. The 3VBM-7 could penetrate 290mm at 2,000m, while the improved 3VBM-7 could penetrate 340mm at the same range. However, the M1A1 had frontal protection equivalent to about 600mm due to its advanced composite armor, and so was not vulnerable to the most common Iraqi ammunition.

Not only did the T-72 offer less armor protection than the M1A1 or Challenger, but it suffered from a distinct vulnerability due to its ammunition layout. The T-72 had 22 rounds of ammunition in its autoloader carousel under the turret, and 17–22 more rounds spread around the hull and turret. When the T-72 was penetrated by an APFSDS or shaped charge projectile, this often led to the ignition of one or more of the ammunition propellant cases exposed in the turret and hull. This in turn caused a chain reaction that eventually ignited the rest of the ammunition, especially that stored in the carousel. The resulting explosion was often great enough to blow the turret off the hull, with it flying into the air. This catastrophic event was not often seen in older Soviet tanks, for several reasons. To begin with, the 125mm gun ammunition used semi-consumable propellant cases that could be much more easily penetrated and ignited than the metal propellant cases used with previous Soviet 100mm and 115mm guns. As importantly, the T-72 contained far more propellant than previous tanks, equivalent to about 450 Megajoules of energy vs 280 Megajoules in the T-62.

The US Army assessed Iraqi tank losses in the war to be 3,847 of the 4,280 tanks in the KTO at the beginning of the conflict. Other AFV losses were put at "over half" of the original 2,880. As mentioned previously, the Coalition air forces claimed to have knocked out 1,772 tanks up to the start of the ground campaign on February 24, more than 40 percent of the initial Iraqi tank strength. The A-10 attack aircraft was credited with destroying

An overhead view of one of the Al-Faw/Al-Najm Enigma tanks brought back to the United States after the Gulf War.

"Final Option," an M1A1 of F Troop, 3rd Armored Cavalry Regiment, during the ground campaign. This unit used large troop letters instead of the more common chevron insignia for troop identification.

987 tanks and 1,355 APCs, while the AH-64 Apache was credited with 278 tanks and 900 other targets, mainly armored vehicles.

Postwar ground surveys were not especially thorough, but they suggested that the aircraft claims were excessive. A US Marine Corps postwar study concluded that about 90 percent of the armored vehicles destroyed in the I MEF sector in Kuwait were knocked out by ground systems, including APFSDS and HEAT warheads from tanks and antitank missiles such as TOW, and the remaining 10 percent of vehicles "by air-delivered ordnance primarily from attack helicopters." In the US Army's western desert sector, the air kills were assessed somewhat higher, about 15–25 percent.

Coalition tank casualties were very low. The US Army had 23 M1A1 Abrams seriously damaged or destroyed during the fighting, of which nine were total losses. Of these, seven were due to fratricide and two more occurred when tanks were destroyed by their own crews when they became bogged down. Only about seven Abrams were hit by Iraqi gunfire. One was temporarily disabled when a hit near the rear of the turret ignited crew stowage; another may have been disabled by a shot through the thin armor of the engine compartment. No hits penetrated through the frontal armor. One Marine M60A1 was lost due to an antitank mine. The British and French forces lost no tanks in combat, and the Arab tank casualties appear to have been limited to the two Qatari AMX30s lost in the initial fighting at Khafji.

Another critical innovation during Operation *Desert Storm* was the advent of the Global Positioning System (GPS) that permitted tank operations in the featureless desert west of Kuwait. The Iraqis were largely unaware of the impact of this new technology, and as a result doubted that the Coalition could conduct large-scale tank operations in the deep desert. This misjudgment had profound consequences for the ill-fated Iraqi defense of Kuwait in the "Mother of all Battles."

FURTHER READING

The 1991 Gulf War has been extensively covered. The bibliography here primarily lists official and semi-official command histories. There are also many divisional histories, memoirs, technical monographs on the various types of tanks used in the campaign, and photo histories of the war. Although extensively used in preparing this book, they are too numerous to be listed here.

Books

Bourque, Stephen, *Jayhawk!: The VII Corps in the Persian Gulf War*, US Army Center of Military History, Washington, DC (2001)

Dinackus, Thomas, *Order of Battle: Allied Ground Forces of Operation Desert Storm*, Hellgate Press, Central Point, OR (2000)

Malovany, Pesach, *Wars of Modern Babylon: A History of the Iraqi Army from 1921 to 2003*, University Press of Kentucky, Lexington (2017)

Pearce, Nigel, *The Shield and the Sabre: The Desert Rats in the Gulf 1990–1991*, HMSO, London (1992)

Scales, Robert, Jr, *Certain Victory: US Army in the Gulf War*, US Army Chief of Staff, Washington, DC (1993)

Schubert, Frank, *et al.*, *The Whirlwind War*, US Center of Military History, Washington, DC (1995)

Swain, Richard, *Lucky War: Third Army in Desert Storm*, US Army Command and General Staff College, Fort Leavenworth, KS (1994)

Toomey, Charles, *XVIII Airborne Corps in Desert Storm*, Hellgate Press, Central Point, OR (2004)

Westermeyer, Paul, *Al-Khafji 28 January–1 February 1991: US Marines in the Gulf War 1990–1991*, USMC History Division, Quantico, VA (2008)

Westermeyer, Paul, *Liberating Kuwait: US Marines in the Gulf War 1990–1991*, USMC History Division, Quantico, VA (2008)

Woods, Kevin, *The Mother of All Battles: Saddam Hussein's Strategic Plan for the Persian Gulf War*, Naval Institute Press, Annapolis, MD (2014)

Government reports

Armor/Anti-Armor Operations in Southwest Asia, US Marine Corps Research Center, Quantico, VA (1992)

Conduct of the Persian Gulf War: Final Report to Congress, US Department of Defense, Washington, DC (1992)

Desert Shield and Desert Storm: Emerging Observations, US Army Armor Center, Fort Knox, KY (1994)

The Iraqi Army: Organization and Tactics: Handbook 100-91, US National Training Center, Fort Irwin, CA (January 1991)

INDEX

Page numbers in **bold** refer to illustrations and their captions.